Writing Passion Plus

ANNOTATED COLLECTION

Ovid: *Amores, Metamorphoses* Selections, Third Edition (2013)
Writing Passion: A Catullus Reader, Second Edition (2013)
Writing Passion Plus: A Catullus Reader Supplement (2013)

Forthcoming
Horace: Selected *Odes* and *Satire* 1.9, Third Edition
Cicero: *Pro Archia Poeta Oratio*, Third Edition
Cicero: *De Amicitia*, Second Edition
Cicero: *Pro Caelio*, Fourth Edition

Writing Passion Plus

Plus

A Catullus Reader Supplement

RONNIE ANCONA

Bolchazy-Carducci Publishers, Inc.
Mundelein, Illinois USA

Editor: Bridget Dean

Contributing Editors: Laurie Haight Keenan and Laurel Draper

Design & Layout: Adam Phillip Velez

Latin Text: D. F. S. Thomson. *Catullus: Edited with a Textual and Interpretative Commentary*
University of Toronto Press 1997
Reprinted with permission of University of Toronto Press

Writing Passion Plus
A Catullus Reader Supplement

Ronnie Ancona

Bolchazy-Carducci Publishers, Inc.
1570 Baskin Road
Mundelein, Illinois 60060
www.bolchazy.com

Printed in the United States of America
2013
by United Graphics

ISBN 978-0-86516-788-9

Library of Congress Cataloging-in-Publication Data

Catullus, Gaius Valerius.
 Writing passion plus : a Catullus reader : supplement / Ronnie Ancona.
    pages. cm. -- (Annotated collection)
 Includes bibliographical references.
  ISBN 978-0-86516-788-9 (pbk. : alk. paper) 1. Latin language--Readers--Poetry. 2. Elegiac poetry, Latin. 3.
Love poetry, Latin. 4. Epigrams, Latin. 5. Rome--Poetry. I. Ancona, Ronnie, 1951- II. Title. III. Series: Annotated
collection.
 PA6274.A25 2013b
 874'.01--dc23
                                                                                    2013009007

For Charles L. Babcock, beloved mentor
1924–2012

CONTENTS

Preface

This little supplement to my textbook *Writing Passion: A Catullus Reader* (second edition 2013) was designed to expand the number and kind of Catullus poems available to teachers and students. Included are Poems 6, 16, 32, and 57 (52 lines of Latin). It is my hope that well-annotated versions of some of the more sexually explicit and/or political poems will broaden appropriately students' awareness of the Catullan corpus.

I have used the same kind of annotation for these poems as I did in *Writing Passion*. For further details on my approach, the reader can refer to the Prefaces to the first and second editions (both contained in the second edition).

Writing Passion Plus builds upon the work I did for *Writing Passion* and thus I owe a debt once again to all of those I have already thanked in that volume. A few deserve special thanks here: Craig Williams for consultation about some sexual terms, Kathleen Grandinetti Durkin for a useful comment on a vocabulary item, Maria Americo for assistance with updating the Catullan bibliography, Norman Clarius for help with Interlibrary Loan at Hunter College, Steven Cole for computer support and more, the Bryn Mawr College Library for its generous public access, Laurie Haight Keenan, editor of the first edition of *Writing Passion*, for help in thinking about the second edition and this supplement, and Bridget Dean, for bringing the supplement and the second edition to fruition with encouragement, good cheer, and professionalism.

Thanks to my Catullus students at Hunter College and the CUNY Graduate Center with whom reading Catullus is always a treat. A final thanks to Paul Pascal for his occasional lecture on Latin sexual terms at the University of Washington back in the 1970s, which, in retrospect, helped inspire me to make Catullus as readable as possible for others.

Narberth, Pennsylvania
January, 2013

Latin Text
with
Notes and Vocabulary

Catullus 6

In this poem, the whole notion of "speech" is deconstructed, for beds and bodies "talk," while people try unsuccessfully to stay silent, and values are upended as seemingly shameful or uncharming things become the subject matter for charming verse. There is a humorous tone to the poem as Catullus wittily shows that he can make good poetry out of anything. Sandwiched between kiss Poems 5 and 7, Poem 6 interestingly manages to be both highly explicit in sexual language and withholding in terms of the specificity of Flavius' object of desire.

Flavi, delicias tuas Catullo,
ni sint illepidae atque inelegantes,
velles dicere nec tacere posses.
verum nescioquid febriculosi

Meter: Hendecasyllabic

1–17 Notice the structure of the poem: 1–5 (statement introduced by a vocative), 6–11 (explanation, introduced by **nam**), 12–14 (another, introduced by a second **nam**), 15–17 (conclusion, introduced by **quārē**).

1   **Flāvius, Flāvī,** *m.,* Flavius, otherwise unknown

    dēlicia, -ae, *f., (usually in pl.)* pleasure, delight, sweetheart, pet, pet animal, toys, erotic verse

    dēliciās: Neither this word nor **scortī** (5) specify the sex of the individual. The sweetheart's sex is unspecified throughout the poem.

    Catullus, -ī, *m.,* Gaius Valerius Catullus, the poet

2   **sint:** The present subjunctive, as here, is sometimes used in conditionals, instead of the imperfect subjunctive, to refer to present time.

    illepidus, -a, -um, *adj.,* lacking grace or refinement

    inēlegans, inēlegantis, *adj.,* unrefined, inelegant, unattractive

    illepidae atque inēlegantēs: Note the two ELISIONS in a row (the only occurrence of this in the poem). Might this underscore the lack of elegance, by suggesting a faltering kind of speech? Charm and attractiveness are highly valued by Catullus. Cf. **lepidum,** used of Catullus' book, in the first line of Poem 1: **Cui dono lepidum novum libellum?**

3   **velles:** The more expected imperfect subjunctive. Cf. note on **sint** (2) above.

    dīcere: "talk about"

    taceō, tacēre, tacuī, tacitum, be silent, say nothing about

    vellēs ... possēs: Notice the idea that charm and elegance naturally lead to speech.

4   **nescioquis, nescioquid,** *indefinite pron. or adj.,* someone or other, something or other

    febrīculōsus, -a, -um, *adj.,* feverish, prone to fevers

    febrīculōsī: "hot" or "sickly"

5   **scorti diligis: hoc pudet fateri.**
       nam te non viduas iacere noctes
       nequiquam tacitum cubile clamat
       sertis ac Syrio fragrans olivo,
       pulvinusque peraeque et hic et ille
10   **attritus, tremulique quassa lecti**

---

5   **scortum, -ī**, *n.*, prostitute (of either sex)

       febrīculōsī / scortī: partitive genitive after **nescioquid**

       dīligō, dīligere, dīlexī, dīlectum, love, esteem, hold dear, have special regard for

       dīligis: a surprising word after **scortī**, mingling affection and purely sexual interest

       hoc: accusative; direct object of **fatērī**

       pudeō, pudēre, puduī, fill with shame, make ashamed

       pudet: impersonal construction. ELLIPSIS of person shamed (the poem's addressee).

       fateor, fatērī, fassus sum, admit, confess

6   **viduus, -a, -um**, *adj.*, deprived of or lacking a husband, wife, etc.

       viduās: TRANSFERRED EPITHET; agrees grammatically with **noctēs**

       viduās . . . noctēs: acc. of extent of time

7   **nēquīquam**, *adv.*, to no effect, in vain

       tacitus, -a, -um, *adj.*, silent

       cubīle, cubīlis, *n.*, bed, couch

       nēquīquam tacitum cubīle clāmat: OXYMORON and PERSONIFICATION. Speaking ability is given
              to the bed. It is silent in vain (by trying to be silent and not succeeding) and it "shouts." This
              echoes line 3 where Flavius' speech and silence are juxtaposed. Flavius is ashamed to speak,
              but his bed speaks despite him.

8   **serta, -ōrum**, *n. pl.*, chains of flowers, garlands

       Syrius, -a, -um, *adj.*, Syrian

       frāgrans, frāgrantis, *adj.*, fragrant, sweet-smelling

       fragrans: first syllable is short here. The consonants "gr" (mute + liquid) means the syllable can be
              long or short. The bed, PERSONIFIED again, is garlanded and fragrant.

       olīvum, -ī, *n.*, olive oil

9   **pulvīnus, -ī**, *m.*, cushion, pillow

       pulvīnus: The "singular" is made double through the pair of demonstrative adjectives, nicely
              making visual the "dual occupancy" of the bed.

       peraequē, *adv.*, uniformly, to the same extent throughout

       hic: This is not the adverb. It is the noun/adjective, nominative, singular, masculine, scanned long
              here (common in poetry).

10   **attrītus, -a, -um**, *adj.*, worn down by use, worn

       tremulus, -a, -um, *adj.*, trembling, shaky, quivering

       quatiō, quatere, quassum, shake, beat upon

       quassa: TRANSFERRED EPITHET. The bed is what is "literally" shaken.

       lectus, -ī, *m.*, bed, couch (also used for reclining at meals or studying)

argutatio inambulatioque.
nam nil stupra valet, nihil, tacere.
cur? non tam latera effututa pandas,
ni tu quid facias ineptiarum.
15 quare, quidquid habes boni malique,
dic nobis. volo te ac tuos amores
ad caelum lepido vocare versu.

11 **argūtātiō, argūtātiōnis**, f., a creaking

argūtātiō: hapax legomenon; noun related to adjective, **argūtus, -a, -um**, which can mean "shrewd or clever," especially of speech, in addition to "creaking," "melodious," "talkative."

inambulātiō, inambulātiōnis, *f.*, pacing, the action of walking up and down, a promenade

argutatio inambulatioque: The two rather grand nouns make the bed's speaking like that of a Roman orator. There is a mock heroic tone to this line.

12 **nīl = nihil**

nīl . . . nihil: repetition for emphasis; adverbial "not at all"

stuprum, -ī, *n.*, dishonor, shame, illicit sexual intercourse

tacēre: Transitive here with **stupra**, accusative.

13–14 **pandās . . . faciās**: Some scholars take as a contrary-to-fact condition with present subjunctives instead of the expected imperfect subjunctives; others take as a future less vivid condition.

13 **latus, lateris,** *n.*, side, flank

effutuō, effutere, effutuī, effutūtum, wear out with sexual intercourse

pandō, pandere, passum/pansum, spread out, open, disclose

nōn . . . pandās: Not only does Flavius' bed speak of his activities, but so does the sight of his "fucked out" body. One can tell what Flavius has been up to just by looking at him. Sights and sounds have meaning, just as words do.

14 **ineptia, -ae,** *f.* silliness, foolishness, (*pl.*) instances of lack of judgment

15 **quidquid**: recalls **nescioquid** in line 4. Each is followed by a partitive genitive. The opposition of **bonī malīque** recalls the juxtaposition of **dīligis / scortī**, reinforcing the unspecified nature of the relationship (positive? negative? loving? merely sexual?) Is Catullus teasing us with lack of information? Cf. Poem 16, where poetry can be seen as stimulating its readers.

16 **nōbīs**: Notice that the potential audience has grown from Catullus in line 1 to the plural (Catullus and others). This use of the plural leads nicely to the larger world that is already starting to know/will know of Flavius and his loves through Catullus' verse.

volǒ: IAMBIC SHORTENING

amor, amōris, *m.*, love, sexual passion, object of one's love (*usually in pl.*), love affair, act of sex; love PERSONIFIED as the god of love

17 **lepidus, -a, -um,** *adj.*, charming, delightful, witty, amusing

lepidō: recalls **illepidae** in line 2. Charming verse can be written about "uncharming" things.

ad caelum . . . vocāre: "pay high honors to" or "immortalize."

versus, -ūs, *m.*, verse, line of poetry

CATULLUS 16

On a surface level, this poem functions as Catullus' proclamation that his life should not be confused with his poetry. If his poetry seems "soft," that does not mean he is "unmanly." The poem, though, functions as a "super-manly" manifesto, by literally and figuratively telling its audience who the "real man" is. Central to this poem are power relations, activity and passivity, gender, the role of the erotic, the role of poetry, and the role of writer and reader. It is important to remember that "manliness" for the Romans was perceived as a function of playing an "active" sexual role, not by the sex (male or female) of one's partner.

> Pedicabo ego vos et irrumabo,
> Aureli pathice et cinaede Furi,
> qui me ex versiculis meis putastis,

Meter: Hendecasyllabic

1–14 Notice the structure of the poem: lines 1–4, 5–11, 12–14.

1   **pēdīcō, pēdīcāre, pēdīcāvī, pēdīcātum**, sexually penetrate anally, sometimes with added sense of threat or humiliation

     irrumō, irrumāre, irrumāvī, irrumātum, sexually penetrate orally, often with hostile sense

     Pedicabo . . . irrumabo: Notice the word order: **ego** is juxtaposed with and "pursuing" **vōs**, reinforcing the aggressive stance of the poem. The "you plural" is surrounded by first person singular verbs that have a dominating sense. The verbs and pronouns form a CHIASTIC pattern, A B B A. Scholars differ on how literally or metaphorically to take the strong verbs of line 1. But maybe that's the point? One should not "choose," but should allow the poem to function as both literal threat and more generalized statement.

2   **Aurēlius, Aurēlī**, *m.*, Aurelius; not identified outside of Catullus' poems. The names of the addressees in the vocative frame line 2 and are visually "beneath" the dominating verbs of line 1. Catullus repeats the CHIASTIC structure from line 1, with names and descriptions forming the A B B A pattern.

     Furius and Aurelius are also the addresses of Poem 11. There they are called his "comrades" and Catullus calls upon them to deliver his farewell to his girlfriend. They appear elsewhere in the Poems as well.

     pathicus, -a, -um, *adj.*, playing the receptive or "submissive" sexual role, especially in anal sex

     cinaedus, -a, -um, *adj.*, effeminate, liable to play the receptive or "submissive" sexual role, shameless, sluttish

     Fūrius, Fūrī, *m.*, Furius; may be the poet Furius Bibaculus

3–4 Understand **esse** in the indirect statement introduced by **putāstis**.

     Furius and Aurelius think Catullus is not manly enough because his verses are somewhat unmanly.

3   **versiculus, -ī**, *m.*, a short line of writing or verse; *pl.*, often poetry of a light or epigrammatic nature

     putāstis: syncopated form of **putāvistis**

> quod sunt molliculi, parum pudicum.
> 5   nam castum esse decet pium poetam
> ipsum, versiculos nihil necesse est;
> qui tum denique habent salem ac leporem,
> si sunt molliculi ac parum pudici,
> et quod pruriat incitare possunt,
> 10   non dico pueris, sed his pilosis

4   **molliculus, -a, -um,** *adj.,* soft, tender, delicate, somewhat unmanly

     parum, *n. indecl. and adv.,* too little, not enough

     pudīcus, -a, -um, *adj.,* having a sense of modesty or shame, modest, honorable, chaste

     pudīcum: In this context, the word has the sense of "sexually inviolate" or "not playing a receptive sexual role."

5–6   Here Catullus sets up the distinction between his verses and himself, as poet (**poētam / ipsum**). The first and last lines of the poem, though, speak in the first person (the "poet"), yet they are poetry. The distinction blurs.

5   **castus, -a, -um,** *adj.,* pure, virgin, sexually faithful, sexually pure, free of vice

     decet, decēre, decuit, *impers. verb,* be right or fitting for, become

     pius, -a, -um, *adj.,* dutiful, devoted, upright

     poēta, -ae, *m.,* poet

6–11   So, how is Catullus' poetry characterized? What does it "do"? It's witty and charming, tender, somewhat unmanly, not sufficiently "chaste," and sexually stimulating to "hairy" (super-masculine?) men, thus making the readers (recipients) somewhat feminized. Thus part of Catullus' defense is that his sexy "unmanly" poetry in fact plays an "active" role. (Writing can be seen variously as an active process where reader *receives* from writer and a passive process where reader is required to actively *create* meaning from a text.) Catullus is playing with his readers by (doubly?) gendering this process. If his verses are "unmanly" – watch out because they are "unmanning" you!

6   **versiculōs . . . est:** Understand **esse** from line 5.

     nihil: adverbial "not at all"

     necesse, *adv.,* necessary

7   **quī:** refers to the verses in line 6

     sāl, salis, *m.,* salt, wit

     lepos, lepōris, *m.,* charm, grace, attractiveness, wit

9   **quod prūriat:** relative clause of characteristic

     prūriō, prūrīre, itch, have a sexual craving, be sexually excited

     incitō, incitāre, incitāvī, incitātum, incite, urge on, arouse

     incitāre: Cf. the use of this word in Poem 2, where Catullus' **puella** arouses sharp bites from her pet bird, the **passer** (lines 3–4). She provokes response just as Catullus' verses do.

10   **puer, puerī,** *m.,* boy, nonadult male, male beloved, (young) male slave

     pilōsus, -a, -um, *adj.,* hairy, covered with hair, shaggy

qui duros nequeunt movere lumbos.
vos, quod milia multa basiorum
legistis, male me marem putatis?
pedicabo ego vos et irrumabo.

11   dūrus, -a, -um, *adj.,* hard, harsh

nequeō, nequīre, nequīvī/nequiī, be unable

lumbus, -ī, *m., usu. pl.* the loins, the area around the hips (as the seat of sexual excitement)

12–13   The question in these lines echoes the sentiment expressed in lines 3–4.

12   mille, *indecl. n. and adj.,* a thousand; *pl.,* mīlia

bāsium, bāsī, *n.,* kiss

bāsiōrum: Catullus uses this word (and/or its related verb for "kiss") in Poems 5 and 7, addressed to the female Lesbia and in Poems 48 and 99, addressed to the male Juventius. The words mīlia multa are an exact repeat from Poem 5, line 10. Most scholars see both sets of "kiss poems" as relevant here.

13   legō, legere, lēgī, lectum, gather, collect, read, recite

male, *adv.,* badly, insufficiently, wickedly, scarcely, awfully

mās, maris, *adj.,* masculine, male, manly, virile

marem: Do not confuse with mare, maris *n.,* "sea."

14   Notice the exact repetition of line 1 as the poem's concluding line.

CATULLUS 32

The poem starts with **amābō**. *The last line reveals the urgency of the literal sense of that word, while the beginning develops the request it initiates in its idiomatic sense. The speaker asks to be invited over and tells his girl how to prepare and what to expect. The poem builds to a surprising and humorous climax. Compare Poem 13 for another "invitation poem" with a surprise ending containing a striking image.*

> **Amabo, mea dulcis ipsimilla,**
> **meae deliciae, mei lepores,**
> **iube ad te veniam meridiatum.**
> **et si iusseris, illud adiuvato,**

Meter: Hendecasyllabic

1–11 The structure consists of 3 lines, then 5 lines, then 3 lines.

1   **amābō**: (often with the addition of **tē**) idiomatic for "please," but the more literal sense (love/ make love to) is present too, considering the content of the poem!

      dulcis, -e, *adj.*, sweet, (of persons) dear, beloved

      ipsimilla: there are difficulties with the manuscript reading. Thomson (1997) provides the reading given here. This word would be a diminutive of "**ipsima**," a quasi-superlative of "**ipsa**" (she herself, mistress of a household, the very one). Take as something like "dear one." Some read "**Ipsitilla**" as a proper name.

2   **dēlicia, -ae**, *f.*, *(usually in pl.)* pleasure, delight, sweetheart, pet, pet animal, toys, erotic verse

      lepos, lepōris, *m.*, charm, grace, attractiveness, wit

3   **iubeō, iubēre, iussī, iussum**, order, command, bid, ask

      iubeō + subjunctive (**veniam**), "order/ask that I come" with or without (as here) **ut**.

      merīdior, merīdiārī, merīdiātus sum, also **merīdiō** etc. (not deponent), take a siesta. Clearly here the siesta will be a lively one!

      merīdiātum: supine in **-um** expressing purpose after verb of motion

4   **iusseris**: repetition of the same verb again in line 9

      illud: "the situation"

      adiuvō, adiuvāre, adiūvī, adiūtum, help, promote, facilitate

      adiuvātō: future imperative, 2nd person singular. The future imperative is primarily used when there is specific reference to future time, as well as in wills, sayings, laws, treaties, etc.

5   **ne quis liminis obseret tabellam,**
           neu tibi lubeat foras abire,
           sed domi maneas paresque nobis
           novem continuas fututiones.
           verum si quid ages, statim iubeto:
10   **nam pransus iaceo et satur supinus**
           pertundo tunicamque palliumque.

---

5   **nē . . . obseret, neu . . . lubeat . . . maneās parēs**: two things not to do and two things to do; optative subjunctives

      quis: perhaps a household slave

      līmen, līminis, *n.*, threshold

      obserō, obserāre, obserāvī, obserātum, bar access to, shut

      tabella, -ae, *f.*, flat piece of wood, tablet, picture, wooden writing tablet usually coated with wax
      tabellam: here, door panel

6   **neu**, *conj.*, and that . . . not

      lubet (libet), lubēre, libuit/libitum est, *impers. verb*, it is pleasing or agreeable

      forās, *adv.*, out, to the outside, outdoors

7   **domī**: locative

      parō, parāre, parāvī, parātum, prepare, ready, get ready, make preparations for

      nōbīs: an indication of intended mutuality

8   **continuus, -a, -um**, *adj.*, continuous, uninterrupted

      futūtiō, futūtiōnis, *f.*, fucking, screwing, copulation

      futūtiōnēs: hapax legomenon. **Futuō, futuere, futuī, futūtum**, the verb from which this noun is derived, generally indicates the action of a man vaginally penetrating a woman. While the verb belongs to explicit Latin vocabulary, it does not, generally, carry the sometimes negative sense of the English "fuck," as in "get the better of" etc. The plural noun lends a mock heroic tone "fuckifications" or "screwifications," which the "nine times in a row" reinforces.

9   **sī quid agēs**: "If you're up for this" or "if you will 'do' something" (**agō** can have sexual connotations).

      iubētō: future imperative. See line 4 above.

10   **prandeō, prandēre, prandī, pransum**, eat the morning or midday meal, lunch

      pransus: perfect passive participle with active meaning

      satur, satura, saturum, *adj.*, well-fed

      supīnus, -a, -um, *adj.*, lying face upwards, lying flat on one's back, passive, languid, supine

      satur supīnus: ASYNDETON

11   **pertundō, pertundere, pertudī, pertūsum**, bore a hole through, perforate

      Note the contrast between his "passive" position on his back and the "action" described. This humorous, exaggerated image, in proleptic fashion, anticipates his later "epic" visit and actions.

      Pertunda, -ae, *f.*, the goddess who presides over the penetration of the hymen.

      tunica, -ae, *f.*, tunic, standard piece of clothing for men or women worn alone or under another garment.

      pallium, -ī, *n.*, outer garment worn by men

      tunicamque palliumque: Polysyndeton reinforces the effect of exaggeration.

Catullus 57

Using sexually explicit language in the service of invective, the speaker attacks Julius Caesar and his subordinate, Mamurra. We know from Suetonius Divus Iulius 73 *that Caesar considered Catullus' verses [unspecified] to have permanently hurt his reputation, but that when Catullus apologized, Caesar invited him to dinner and that Caesar kept up his friendship with Catullus' father. We do not know which of Catullus' verses occasioned this reaction, but the information from Suetonius provides an interesting window onto the not-so-separate arenas of literature and politics in Catullus' time.*

> Pulcre convenit improbis cinaedis,
> Mamurrae pathicoque Caesarique.
> nec mirum: maculae pares utrisque

Meter: Hendecasyllabic

1   **pulcrē**, *adv.*, beautifully, perfectly, thoroughly

    conveniō, convenīre, convēnī, conventum, meet, agree with; *impers.* it is agreed

    convenit: The short "e" indicated by the meter makes this present tense, not perfect.

    pulcrē convenit + dat.: "they get along very well together"; dative plurals in line 1, and then "naming" dative singulars in line 2

    improbus, -a, -um, *adj.*, morally unsound, unprincipled, shameless, greedy, flagrant

    cinaedus, -ī, *m.*, one who is effeminate, liable to play the receptive or "submissive" sexual role, shameless, sluttish

2   **Māmurra, -ae**, *m.*, Mamurra, from Formiae, officer of engineers under Caesar in Spain and Gaul where he became very wealthy and spent a lot. He and his girlfriend are attacked by Catullus in other poems as well. In several, he is referred to as **Mentula**, "Prick."

    pathicus, -a, -um, *adj.*, playing the receptive or "submissive" sexual role, especially in anal sex

    -que . . . -que: The positioning is unusual. Most take the adjective **pathicō** as applying to both Mamurra and Caesar.

    Caesar, Caesaris, *m.*, Julius Caesar, the famous Roman general and politician, 100–44 BCE; friend of Catullus' family; attacked by Catullus in several poems.

3   **mīrus, -a, -um**, *adj.*, amazing, remarkable, astonishing

    nec mīrum: understand **est**

    macula, -ae, *f.*, stain, spot, blemish, sign of disgrace

    pār, paris, *adj.*, equal, matching, even

    uterque, utraque, utrumque, *adj., pron.*, each of two

    utrīsque: used in plural here, most often used in singular

urbana altera et illa Formiana,
5   impressae resident nec eluentur:
morbosi pariter, gemelli utrique,
uno in lecticulo erudituli ambo,
non hic quam ille magis vorax adulter,
rivales socii et puellularum.
10   pulcre convenit improbis cinaedis.

---

4   **urbānus, -a, -um,** *adj.,* connected with or of the city (especially, Rome), elegant and sophisticated

altera and **illa:** each refers to a **macula**

urbāna ... Formiāna: CHIASMUS A B B A

Formiānus, -a, -um, *adj.,* of or belonging to Formiae, city on the coast of Latium

5   **imprimō, imprimere, impressī, impressum,** press, stamp, imprint

impressae: nominative plural feminine, refers to **maculae**

resideō, residēre, resēdī, remain seated, remain in existence, persist

ēluō, ēluere, ēluī, ēlūtum, wash clean, erase

6   **morbōsus, -a, -um,** *adj.,* unhealthy, sickly, morbidly lustful

pariter, *adv.,* side by side, together, equally, alike, simultaneously

gemellus, -a, -um, *adj.,* twin, double, like, having the characteristics of twins; the ELISION of **gemellī utrīque** reinforces the sense.

7   **lecticulus, -ī,** *m.,* bed, couch (diminutive of **lectus**)

ērudītulus, -a, -um, *adj.,* learned, accomplished (diminutive of **ērudītus**)

ērudītulī: Caesar, of course, was author and stylist. The two-line epigram, Poem 105, attacks Mamurra's literary pretensions. Since **lecticulus** can refer to a bed for sleeping or a study couch, it neatly suggests that their so-called "erudition" encompasses both sex and writing. The tone of the diminutives is contemptuous.

ambō, ambae, ambō, *pl. adj. and pron.,* both

ūnō in ... ambō: The three ELISIONS in this line "join" the pair on the bed/couch. The play on "oneness" and "double-ness" frames the line.

8   **vorax, vorācis,** *adj.,* ravenous, insatiable

adulter, adulterī, *m.,* illicit or clandestine lover, adulterer

9   **rīvālis, -is,** *m., f.,* rival

socius, -a, -um, *adj.,* living or acting in partnership, shared, common

puellula, -ae, *f.,* (young) girl

rīvālēs sociī ... puellārum: Even their rivalry is "shared." For the Romans, being a womanizer and being a **cinaedus** were not incompatible. Both suggest a state of out-of-control or deviant behavior and accusations of being either or both were typical parts of invective.

10   Line 10 repeats exactly line 1. Cf. the same kind of repetition in Poem 16.

Latin Text without Notes and Vocabulary

Catullus 6

Flavi, delicias tuas Catullo,
ni sint illepidae atque inelegantes,
velles dicere nec tacere posses.
verum nescioquid febriculosi
5   scorti diligis: hoc pudet fateri.
nam te non viduas iacere noctes
nequiquam tacitum cubile clamat
sertis ac Syrio fragrans olivo,
pulvinusque peraeque et hic et ille
10   attritus, tremulique quassa lecti
argutatio inambulatioque.
nam nil stupra valet, nihil, tacere.
cur? non tam latera effututa pandas,
ni tu quid facias ineptiarum.
15   quare, quidquid habes boni malique,
dic nobis. volo te ac tuos amores
ad caelum lepido vocare versu.

CATULLUS 16

Pedicabo ego vos et irrumabo,
Aureli pathice et cinaede Furi,
qui me ex versiculis meis putastis,
quod sunt molliculi, parum pudicum.
5   nam castum esse decet pium poetam
ipsum, versiculos nihil necesse est;
qui tum denique habent salem ac leporem,
si sunt molliculi ac parum pudici,
et quod pruriat incitare possunt,
10   non dico pueris, sed his pilosis
qui duros nequeunt movere lumbos.
vos, quod milia multa basiorum
legistis, male me marem putatis?
pedicabo ego vos et irrumabo.

CATULLUS 32

Amabo, mea dulcis ipsimilla,
meae deliciae, mei lepores,
iube ad te veniam meridiatum.
et si iusseris, illud adiuvato,
5   ne quis liminis obseret tabellam,
neu tibi lubeat foras abire,
sed domi maneas paresque nobis
novem continuas fututiones.
verum si quid ages, statim iubeto:
10   nam pransus iaceo et satur supinus
pertundo tunicamque palliumque.

Catullus 57

Pulcre convenit improbis cinaedis,
Mamurrae pathicoque Caesarique.
nec mirum: maculae pares utrisque,
urbana altera et illa Formiana,
5   impressae resident nec eluentur:
morbosi pariter, gemelli utrique,
uno in lecticulo erudituli ambo,
non hic quam ille magis vorax adulter,
rivales socii et puellularum.
10   pulcre convenit improbis cinaedis.

VOCABULARY

In general, only long vowels in metrically indeterminate positions are marked. For example, the length of the *a* in "annus" need not be marked as long or short because the syllable in which it is contained must be long, regardless of the length of the vowel, because the vowel is followed by two consonants, "nn," (not a combination like *tr* which can create indeterminacy), while the *a* in "beātus" must be marked long because it occurs in a position where metrical rules cannot determine the length of the syllable in which it occurs. Genitive singular of second declension nouns whose nominative singular ends in "-ius" or "-ium" is given as *ī* (not *iī*) since that was the form in use when Catullus wrote. These words have the whole word written in the genitive rather than just *ī*, e.g., "Cornelius, Cornelī" vs. "scriptum, -ī." These genitives accent the penult, even when short. The same holds for the accent in the vocative of second declension proper names ending in "-ius," e.g., "Cornélī."

A

adiuvō, adiuvāre, adiūvī, adiūtum, help, promote, facilitate

adulter, adulterī, *m.,* illicit or clandestine lover, adulterer

ambō, ambae, ambō, *pl. adj. and pron.,* both

amor, amōris, *m.,* love, sexual passion, object of one's love *(usually in pl.),* love affair, act of sex; love PERSONIFIED as the god of love

argūtātiō, argūtātiōnis, *f.,* a creaking

attrītus, -a, -um, *adj.,* worn down by use, worn

Aurēlius, Aurēlī, *m.,* Aurelius; not identified outside of Catullus' poems.

B

bāsium, bāsī, *n.,* kiss

C

Caesar, Caesaris, *m.,* Julius Caesar, the famous Roman general and politician, 100–44 BCE; friend of Catullus' family; attacked by Catullus in several poems.

castus, -a, -um, *adj.,* pure, virgin, sexually faithful, sexually pure, free of vice

Catullus, -ī, *m.,* Gaius Valerius Catullus, the poet

cinaedus, -a, -um, *adj.,* effeminate, liable to play the receptive or "submissive" sexual role, shameless, sluttish

cinaedus, -ī, *m.*, one who is effeminate, liable to play the receptive or "submissive" sexual role, shameless, sluttish

continuus, -a, -um, *adj.*, continuous, uninterrupted

conveniō, convenīre, convēnī, conventum, meet, agree with; *impers.* it is agreed

cubīle, cubīlis, *n.*, bed, couch

D

decet, decēre, decuit, *impers. verb,* be right or fitting for, become

dēlicia, -ae, *f., (usually in pl.)* pleasure, delight, sweetheart, pet, pet animal, toys, erotic verse

dīligō, dīligere, dīlexī, dīlectum, love, esteem, hold dear, have special regard for

dulcis, -e, *adj.*, sweet, (of persons) dear, beloved

dūrus, -a, -um, *adj.*, hard, harsh

E

effutuō, effutere, effutuī, effutūtum, wear out with sexual intercourse

ēluō, ēluere, ēluī, ēlūtum, wash clean, erase

ērudītulus, -a, -um, *adj.*, learned, accomplished (diminutive of ērudītus)

F

fateor, fatērī, fassus sum, admit, confess

febrīculōsus, -a, -um, *adj.*, feverish, prone to fevers

Flāvius, Flāvī, *m.*, Flavius, otherwise unknown

forās, *adv.*, out, to the outside, outdoors

Formiānus, -a, -um, *adj.*, of or belonging to Formiae, city on the coast of Latium.

frāgrans, frāgrantis, *adj.*, fragrant, sweet-smelling

Fūrius, Fūrī, *m.*, Furius; may be the poet Furius Bibaculus

futūtiō, futūtiōnis, *f.*, fucking, screwing, copulation

G

gemellus, -a, -um, *adj.*, twin, double, like, having the characteristics of twins

I

illepidus, -a, -um, *adj.*, lacking grace or refinement

imprimō, imprimere, impressī, impressum, press, stamp, imprint

improbus, -a, -um, *adj.*, morally unsound, unprincipled, shameless, greedy, flagrant

inambulātiō, inambulātiōnis, *f.*, pacing, the action of walking up and down, a promenade

incitō, incitāre, incitāvī, incitātum, incite, urge on, arouse

inēlegans, inēlegantis, *adj.*, unrefined, inelegant, unattractive

ineptia, -ae, *f.*, silliness, foolishness, *(pl.)* instances of lack of judgment

irrumō, irrumāre, irrumāvī, irrumātum, sexually penetrate orally, often with hostile sense

iubeō, iubēre, iussī, iussum, order, command, bid, ask

L

latus, lateris, *n.*, side, flank

lecticulus, -ī, *m.*, bed, couch (diminutive of **lectus**)

lectus, -ī, *m.*, bed, couch (also used for reclining at meals or studying)

legō, legere, lēgī, lectum, gather, collect, read, recite

lepidus, -a, -um, *adj.*, charming, delightful, witty, amusing

lepos, lepōris, *m.*, charm, grace, attractiveness, wit

lepos, lepōris, *m.*, charm, grace, attractiveness, wit

līmen, līminis, *n.*, threshold

lubet (libet), lubēre, libuit/libitum est, *impers. verb,* it is pleasing or agreeable

lumbus, -ī, *m., usu. pl.* the loins, the area around the hips (as the seat of sexual excitement)

M

macula, -ae, *f.*, stain, spot, blemish, sign of disgrace

male, *adv.*, badly, insufficiently, wickedly, scarcely, awfully

Māmurra, -ae, *m.*, Mamurra, from Formiae, officer of engineers under Caesar in Spain and Gaul where he became very wealthy and spent a lot.

mās, maris, *adj.*, masculine, male, manly, virile

merīdior, merīdiārī, merīdiātus sum, also merīdiō etc. (not deponent), take a siesta.

mille, *indecl. n. and adj.*, a thousand; *pl.*, mīlia

mīrus, -a, -um, *adj.*, amazing, remarkable, astonishing

molliculus, -a, -um, *adj.*, soft, tender, delicate, somewhat unmanly

morbōsus, -a, -um, *adj.*, unhealthy, sickly, morbidly lustful

N

necesse, *adv.*, necessary

nequeō, nequīre, nequīvī/nequiī, be unable

nēquiquam, *adv.*, to no effect, in vain

nescioquis, nescioquid, *indefinite pron. or adj.*, someone or other, something or other

neu, *conj.*, and that . . . not

O

obserō, obserāre, obserāvī, obserātum, bar access to, shut

olīvum, -ī, *n.*, olive oil

P

pallium, -ī, *n.*, outer garment worn by men

pandō, pandere, passum/pansum, spread out, open, disclose

pār, paris, *adj.*, equal, matching, even

pariter, *adv.*, side by side, together, equally, alike, simultaneously

parō, parāre, parāvī, parātum, prepare, ready, get ready, make preparations for

parum, *n. indecl. and adv.*, too little, not enough

pathicus, -a, -um, *adj.*, playing the receptive or "submissive" sexual role, especially in anal sex

pēdīcō, pēdīcāre, pēdīcāvī, pēdīcātum, sexually penetrate anally, sometimes with added sense of threat or humiliation

peraequē, *adv.*, uniformly, to the same extent throughout

Pertunda, -ae, *f.*, the goddess who presides over the penetration of the hymen

pertundō, pertundere, pertudī, pertūsum, bore a hole through, perforate

pilōsus, -a, -um, *adj.*, hairy, covered with hair, shaggy

pius, -a, -um, *adj.*, dutiful, devoted, upright

poēta, -ae, *m.*, poet

prandeō, prandēre, prandī, pransum, eat the morning or midday meal, lunch

prūriō, prūrīre, itch, have a sexual craving, be sexually excited

pudeō, pudēre, puduī, fill with shame, make ashamed

pudīcus, -a, -um, *adj.*, having a sense of modesty or shame, modest, honorable, chaste

puellula, -ae, *f.*, (young) girl

puer, puerī, *m.*, boy, nonadult male, male beloved, (young) male slave

pulcrē, *adv.*, beautifully, perfectly, thoroughly

pulvīnus, -ī, *m.*, cushion, pillow

Q

quatiō, quatere, quassum, shake, beat upon

R

resideō, residēre, resēdī, remain seated, remain in existence, persist

rīvālis, -is, *m., f.*, rival

S

sāl, salis, *m.*, salt, wit

satur, satura, saturum, *adj.*, well-fed

scortum, -ī, *n.*, prostitute (of either sex)

serta, -ōrum, *n. pl.*, chains of flowers, garlands

socius, -a, -um, *adj.*, living or acting in partnership, shared, common

stuprum, -ī, *n.*, dishonor, shame, illicit sexual intercourse

supīnus, -a, -um, *adj.*, lying face upwards, lying flat on one's back, passive, languid, supine

Syrius, -a, -um, *adj.*, Syrian

T

tabella, -ae, *f.*, flat piece of wood, tablet, picture, wooden writing tablet usually coated with wax

taceō, tacēre, tacuī, tacitum, be silent, say nothing about

tacitus, -a, -um, *adj.*, silent

tremulus, -a, -um, *adj.*, trembling, shaky, quivering

tunica, -ae, *f.*, tunic, standard piece of clothing for men or women worn alone or under another garment.

U

urbānus, -a, -um, *adj.*, connected with or of the city (especially, Rome), elegant and sophisticated

uterque, utraque, utrumque, *adj., pron.*, each of two

V

versiculus, -ī, *m.*, a short line of writing or verse; *pl.*, often poetry of a light or epigrammatic nature

versus, -ūs, *m.*, verse, line of poetry

viduus, -a, -um, *adj.*, deprived of or lacking a husband, wife, etc.

vorax, vorācis, *adj.*, ravenous, insatiable